Wisdom of the Marx Brothers

Life Lessons from Groucho, Chico, and Harpo

Luis Anthony Gonzalez

Introduction

The Marx Brothers were one of a kind. Their comedic style blends zany slapstick with wit and sarcasm. Their films date back nearly a century, but the comedy is timeless. The humor stems from keen observations and commentary on human nature—which never gets old. Humor is unvarnished truth—if it weren't true, it wouldn't be funny. The films of the Marx Brothers offer many funny moments, many truths, many life lessons.

Within these pages you will find a dozen life lessons gleaned from the films and lives of Groucho, Chico and Harpo. May your life by enriched by the Wisdom of the Marx Brothers.

Dedication

This book is dedicated to everyone born March 22, November 23, October 2, and February 29…plus any day in January—you know who you are!

Lesson #1: Don't Go It Alone

"You know what I say. Whenever you got business trouble the best thing to do is to get a lawyer. Then you got more trouble, but at least you got a lawyer."

(Antonio Pirelli (Chico), *At the Circus*)

At the Circus, 1939 Metro-Goldwyn Mayer

Scene Setup: Antonio Pirelli (Chico) walks in on a conversation between Jeff Wilson (Kenny Baker), the circus owner, and Mr. Carter (James Burke), to whom Wilson owes $10,000 and who is trying to swindle Wilson out of ownership of the circus. Pirelli realizes

3

that his friend is in trouble, and he offers the advice of getting a lawyer. Pirelli later takes out his book of contacts and looks under "t' for trouble and finds the name of J. Cheever Loophole, Lawyer (played by Groucho).

The Lesson: Chico realizes that in business (as well as in life) it is best not to go it alone. Savvy business people surround themselves with smart associates. Every businessperson needs a good lawyer, accountant, tech expert, banker, insurance broker, and marketing guru. Further, learn to delegate. Even the best among us cannot do everything. Hire bright associates who can not only do what you do, but can do it better. Another important player is a mentor. A mentor is typically someone with more experience than yourself and who possesses the wisdom that comes from life rather than textbooks. Don't be afraid to ask these folks for advice. In everyday life, the same principles apply: you need a trusted attorney, accountant, banker and insurance broker. The way to find good people is by networking. Talk to as many people as possible. The people you talk to can lead you to the contacts you need. Also, talk to the "sages" in your family—perhaps it's a parent or grandparent, or that aunt or uncle everyone looks up to. Once you find good advisors, hold on to them! And be sure to nurture your relationships by being there for others.

Lesson #2: It Is Best to Bring Extras

"And Two Hard Boiled Eggs"
[Honk]
"Make That Three Hard Boiled Eggs"
(Otis B. Driftwood (Groucho), *A Night at the Opera)*

A Night at the Opera, 1935, Metro-Goldwyn-Mayer

Scene Setup: Aboard a cruise ship, standing outside of a cabin, Otis B. Driftwood (Groucho) is dictating a dinner order to a steward. Unbeknownst to the steward, Driftwood is ordering not only for himself, but for three others inside the cabin. The order is extensive, particularly since Chico continually yells out "and two hard boiled eggs," followed by a honk from Harpo, prompting Groucho to amend the order, "make that three hard boiled eggs."

The Lesson: Groucho is egged on by Chico (pun intended) to add to the order. The wisdom is that it is best to have more than what you think you might need. This goes for many things in life. When leaving for work or going on a trip, bring a bit more money than what you need. Pack that extra underwear and pair of socks on your vacation. Bring a few extra napkins, ketchup packets, etc. with your takeout order. Save more money than what you think you need for the down payment on the house. Give yourself extra time to get places. Often, the "extra" turns out to be just the right amount. This also goes for preparing for an exam. If you think you have studied enough to get an "A," study some more. When working on long-term projects, take the attitude that if you are not going ahead in your work, you are falling behind. Generally, do more than what it expected. That is how you will get noticed and this will propel you to achieve the advancement you seek.

Lesson #3: Know When to Keep Quiet
[Honk!]
(Harpo)

Pictorial Parade, 1935

Scene Setup: In more than a dozen films, Harpo manages to utter not a single word; yet, he speaks volumes.

The Lesson: Harpo knew that opening one's mouth can lead to trouble. It has been said that we have two ears and just one mouth so that we can listen twice as much as we speak. It has also been said that it is better to remain silent and be thought a fool, than to open one's mouth and remove all doubt. Additionally, loose lips sink ships. Of course, you cannot spend your entire life honking and whistling. At some point, you may have to say something. A good piece of advice is to think about what you are going to say three times in your head (and think about what the reaction might be) before you say anything. Words, particularly said in haste or anger, can do great harm. A well-crafted utterance, on the other hand, can change a life for the better. So, be cautious. And, when in doubt, stay quiet.

Chico's wife, Betty, could have used this lesson. According to Maxine Marx (Chico's daughter and author of *Growing Up with Chico),* Betty once encouraged Chico to negotiate more camera time for their upcoming film, *A Day at the Races*. Betty felt that Groucho upstaged Chico. Chico, likely fueled by jealousy, confronted his brothers. When he returned home, Chico was furious with Betty for making the suggestion. He told her, "Next time, keep your ideas to yourself. You almost broke up the Marx Brothers."

Lesson #4: Take Care of Your Future

"Oh, I know it's a penny here and a penny there, but look at me. I worked myself up from nothing to a state of extreme poverty."
(Groucho, *Monkey Business*)

Monkey Business, 1931, Paramount Pictures

Scene Setup: A stowaway on a cruise ship, Groucho is trying to convince mobster Joe Helton (Rockcliffe Fellowes) to hire him as his new bodyguard. Groucho is using a nonsensical economic argument. Helton will think it over.

The Lesson: Nonsense or not, Groucho is thinking about his future. He is putting forth his own version of "a penny saved is a penny earned." In real life, Groucho (who grew up in poverty) was known to have been concerned about money. He said, "As I grew successful, the one thing that continually haunted me was the fear of being destitute in my old age. "He lost a great deal of money in the stock market crash of 1929. He was able to bounce back from that loss by making sound investments and thinking about his future (which is more than can be said about Chico, who was a gambler). Money is by no means the be all and end all; it is, however, beneficial. Groucho once quipped: "While money can't buy happiness, it certainly lets you choose your own form of misery." It is important to save for a rainy day (or a monsoon). Life is sometimes unpredictable and you don't want poor financial planning to add to your misery.

Lesson #5: Read the Fine Print

"Now pay particular attention to this first clause because it's most important. It says the, uh… 'The party of the first part shall be known in this contract as the party of the first part.' *How do you like that? That's pretty neat, eh?"*

(Otis B. Driftwood (Groucho), *A Night at the Opera)*

A Night at the Opera, 1935, Metro-Goldwyn-Mayer

Scene Setup: Driftwood (Groucho) is reviewing a contract with Fiorello (Chico). The fact that the contract is written in legal jargon is further complicated by the fact that Fiorello can't read.

The Lesson: Chico is justifiably skeptical of the contract. It pays to be a little paranoid in life. Don't take anything for granted. Read the fine print; get all the details. Don't be afraid to ask questions. Whenever possible, get it in writing. And remember, if something seems too good to be true, it probably is.

Legal matters are usually taken seriously; unless you are one of the Marx Brothers. When Warner Brothers caught wind of the fact that the Marx Brothers were making a film called, *A Night in Casablanca*, they were naturally concerned as to how this might impact their film, *Casablanca*. While Warner Brothers never actually threatened to sue, Groucho took the opportunity to embellish the matter and wrote a famous "response" to Warner Brothers as a publicity stunt. As part of his long-winded searing, Groucho wrote: "You claim you own Casablanca and that no one else can use that name without their permission. What about Warner Brothers— do you own that, too? You probably have the right to use the name Warner, but what about Brothers? Professionally, we were brothers long before you were."

Lesson # 6: Fake It Till You Make It...And Don't Get Caught!

"You don't have to look any further, I've got the most peculiar talents of any doctor you've ever met."

(Dr. Hackenbush (Groucho) *A Day at the Races***)**

A Day at the Races, 1937, Metro-Goldwyn-Mayer

Scene Setup: Hackenbush (Groucho) is actually a horse doctor, but is passing himself off as a medical doctor and is applying to head up a sanitarium.

The Lesson: no one is advocating lying about one's credentials, training, skills, etc. The idea is that we sometimes need to convince ourselves that we can actually do something. It is natural to occasionally doubt our own ability to accomplish a goal or fill a position. This is when we need to persuade our toughest critic (ourselves) that we belong at that school, company or job.

While Groucho was a bit skeptical of the Brothers' ability to make it past vaudeville, Chico never lacked confidence. He had his eye on Broadway, stating, "What have they got on Broadway that we haven't got?" *(Groucho and Me)*.

But you can't fake certain things. Groucho confesses that the brothers were "congenital liars." Chico once got a position as a lifeguard when his swimming abilities were not up to par with job. When he attempted to save a drowning man, both the man and Chico had to be rescued.

Lesson #7: Do Things Your Own Way

"I don't know whether my life has been a success or a failure. But not having any anxiety about becoming one instead of the other, and just taking things as they come along, I've had a lot of extra time to enjoy life."
(Harpo Marx)

Go West, 1940, Metro-Goldwyn-Mayer

The Lesson: Harpo knew a thing or two about doing things his own way. He opted not to speak in films at a time when "talking pictures" were all the rage. He played the harp—not a particularly popular instrument. He did things his own way (much how Chico played the piano). Harpo was very much an original. It has been said that you should be yourself, mostly because everybody else is taken. You get no points for originality by imitating others. Be happy with who you are.

The Marx Brothers were original not only in their act, but in real life as well. In his book, *Harpo Speaks*, Harpo tells the story of how he handled the distraction of a neighbor playing the piano too loudly. The neighbor was Sergei Rachmininoff, a famous Russian pianist and composer. Harpo wrote: "I opened the door and all the windows in my place and began to play the first four bars of Rachmaninoff's Prelude in C-sharp Minor, over and over, fortissimo. Two hours later my fingers were getting numb. But I didn't let up, not until I heard a thunderous crash of notes from across the way, like the keyboard had been attacked with a pair of sledge hammers. Then there was silence."

Lesson #8: Don't Confuse Stupidity for Bravery

"You're a brave man. Go and break through the lines. And remember, while you're out there risking your life and limb through shot and shell, we'll be in be in here thinking what a sucker you are."
(Rufus T. Firefly (Groucho), Duck Soup)

Duck Soup, 1933, Paramount Pictures

Scene Setup: Rufus T. Firefly (Groucho) is the leader of a fledgling country, Freedonia. Freedonia has gone to war against Sylvania. Firefly sends an officer into battle, commending him for his bravery, but actually bringing to light the soldier's foolishness for plunging into harm's way.

The Lesson: There are times in life when we believe that we are called to be brave or noble, when in fact what we are being asked to do is actually stupid. Some fights are worth fighting; others are not. Bravery for a wrong or unjust reason is actually an act of cowardice in that you are afraid to back down.

Lesson #9: Don't Overstay Your Welcome

"Hello, I must be going
I cannot stay, I came to say I must be going
I'm glad I came, but just the same, I must be
going, la-la!"
(Captain Jeffrey Spaulding (Groucho),
Animal Crackers)

Animal Crackers, 1930, Paramount Pictures

Scene Setup: Mrs. Rittenhouse (Margaret Dumont) is throwing a gala in honor of Captain Spaulding (Groucho), who has returned from exploring Africa. Spaulding informs Rittenhouse that he cannot stay.

The Lesson: Benjamin Franklin once said that guests, like fish, begin to smell after three days. Even the most welcomed and charming of guests start to get on your nerves after a while. This can also hold true in a job. The worker who was once the darling of the company can become yesterday's news after a few years. You might say that the bloom is off the rose. Show yourself the door and head to a new adventure before someone pushes you out.
As the famous song says:
"Hello, I must be going
I cannot stay, I came to say
I must be going
I'm glad I came, But just the same
I must be going, la-la!"

Lesson #10: Don't Get In Over Your Head

"My good man, statistics prove it costs five dollars a week to provide for a child. Twelve times five is sixty dollars. You only make twenty-five dollars a week! It's economically impossible for you to have twelve children!" (Wolf J. Flywheel (Groucho), *The Big Store*)

The Big Store, 1941, Metro-Goldwyn-Mayer

Scene Setup: Giuseppi (Henry Armetta) is in the store and can only find six of his 12 children. Flywheel (Groucho) asks him how much money he makes a week.

The man explains that he makes $25. Flywheel concludes that the man can't possibly have 12 kids because he cannot afford that many children.

The Lesson: It is easy to get caught in the trap of keeping up with the Joneses—the notion that, if our neighbors buy something, we should buy it too. If they get a new car, we should get a new car. If they get a swimming pool, we should get a swimming pool; and so forth. The problem is that, perhaps, the Jones family can afford such luxuries—and we cannot. Credit cards and home equity loans make it all too easy to buy those things we actually can't afford. Before we know it, we are in over our heads in debt. Don't fall for the trap. Create a sensible budget and stick with it.

Lesson #11: Be Grateful, Be Charitable

"I ain't got nothing, but you can always have half!"

(Antonio Perilli (Chico), *At the Circus*)

At the Circus, 1939, Metro-Goldwyn-Mayer

Scene Setup: Perilli (Chico) feels bad for his friend, Jeff Wilson (Kenny Baker), the circus owner, who might lose the circus if he doesn't come up with enough money to pay off a loan. Perilli is willing to give Wilson half of everything he has—which, unfortunately, is nothing.

The Lesson: No doubt Chico is grateful. His statement expresses gratitude. Either gratitude towards his friend or simply gratitude in general. There are times in life when gratitude compels us to action, to somehow return what we have received. Sometimes we pay it back to those who have helped us out; other times we pay it forward. Paying it forward means doing for others what someone has done for you. Paying it forward extends and perpetuates love and charity. The grateful person is a charitable person. Charity can be in the form of time, talent or treasure. You might give a monetary donation, you might help feed the hungry, or you might simply share a laugh and a smile when it is needed most. Be grateful for what you have (don't worry about what you don't), give freely of yourself, and you will be a happy individual.

Lesson #12: Live, Love, Laugh, Gooki

*"Why, you've got beauty, charm, money! You
have got money, haven't you? Because if you
haven't, we can quit right now."*
(Captain Jeffrey Spaulding (Groucho),
***Animal Crackers*)**

Animal Crackers, 1930, Paramount Pictures

Scene Setup: Captain Spaulding (Groucho) is trying to
charm Mrs. Whitehead and Mrs. Rittenhouse. He is
flattering them but, at the same time, he wants to be sure
that they possess the one thing he is really looking for—
money.

The Lesson: Groucho (in his usual witty sarcasm) is highlighting those superficial qualities (beauty, charm, wealth) that people get caught up in. In truth, none of these things bring true happiness. True happiness comes from living a purposeful life. Studies on longevity consistently cite living a purposeful life as one of the keys to a long (and happy) life. True happiness comes from loving others, caring for others. The selfish person, the jealous person, can never truly be happy. True happiness comes from laughing. Laughter, they say, is the best medicine. Research shows that laughter boosts your immunity, decreases your stress hormones and helps you fight diseases. Laughter also produces endorphins— your brain's feel-good chemicals. The Gooki, Harpo's signature funny face, can be seen as a facial yoga of sorts. In addition to producing laughter and releasing stress, it is just down right fun. So, live, love, laugh, gooki.

Monkey Business, 1931, Paramount Pictures

43900955R00021